RITE OF BAPTISM FOR CHILDREN

Arranged for Communal Participation

The Rite for Several Children and for One Child

With the People's Parts of the Rite
Printed in **Boldface Type**

Edited by
Rev. Victor Hoagland, C.P.

CATHOLIC BOOK PUBLISHING CO.
New York, N.Y.

Concordat cum originali:
Ronald F. Krisman, Executive Director
Secretariat for the Liturgy
National Conference of Catholic Bishops

Approved by the National Conference of Catholic Bishops for use in the dioceses of the United States of America, 13 November 1969. Confirmed by decree of the Congregation for Divine Worship, 5 January 1970 (Prot. N. CD 1887/69).

Published by authority of the Committee on the Liturgy, National Conference of Catholic Bishops.

(T-80)

Printed in U.S.A.

CONTENTS

LETTER TO NEW PARENTS

YOUR child is born. What joy you must feel! The moment you held the infant in your arms you may have wondered: "What will our child become?

In some way, the answer depends on you, for the child is yours.

Who Is This Child of Yours?

By baptizing your child, you decide that your baby will be a Christian, a member of Christ's body, the Church. You could not choose anything more precious.

By baptizing your child you recognize your child is a child of God, with a lifelong mission prepared for her or him. You put your dear one in God's hands in this sacrament and commit your child to the loving care of Jesus Christ, God's Son.

Your child is our child too. As you gather family, friends and neighbors to celebrate this new life, you invite others to help your child on life's journey. "The village raises the child," says an old African maxim. At baptism you introduce your child to the wider human family.

Your child is also a child of earth. Sun and moon, sky and sea welcome this child of yours. At baptism you hold your little one and say: "Child of God, human child, live peacefully on this planet of ours."

Teaching Your Child God's Ways

Learn the wonderful mystery that takes place when your child is baptized from the signs and words of the sacrament itself. It has a simple, quiet language all its own.

During the baptismal ceremony, for example, you carry your child, you speak its name, you listen, answer, and pray for your little one. In your role as parents you will do these things again and again, initiating your child into the ways of human life.

As parents you are your child's first teachers of faith. You will bring your child to church; from you your son or daughter will learn day by day to hear the word of God, to pray, and to love God and neighbor. Can anyone better than you teach your child how to love the world God created? To trust in the goodness of life? To feel loved and wanted?

Commit yourselves, with God's grace, to this holy task as your child is baptized.

Godparents stand beside you during baptism as a sign that this great work is not yours alone. Other faithful Christians will also teach, pray for, and be models for your child. In choosing godparents, therefore, the Church asks you to choose people of faith.

The whole Christian community, represented during the ceremony by the celebrant, promises to offer your son or daughter its powerful support.

The Sign of the Cross, the Readings and the Prayers

Following the initial greeting, you sign your child's forehead with the Sign of the Cross, an ancient Christian gesture that designates your child a follower of Jesus Christ.

God's word in Scripture is then read, in which you will hear Jesus encouraging you in your responsibilities. The readings are followed by prayers for your child, for families, and for the Church. The saints, especially your child's patron saint, are asked to intercede for you.

Then the celebrant of baptism, relying on the power of Jesus, prays that your child may be free from the power of evil and made a holy temple of God.

At the Baptismal Font

Carrying your child, you then go to where the baptism will take place.

The sacraments bring those who believe to Jesus Christ. By simple signs of water and words, Jesus who said, "Let the children come to me," invites your child to share the great mysteries of his life.

Jesus once entered the waters of the Jordan and was baptized by John. The heavens opened and God acknowledged him as his Son. The Spirit rested on him and led him on his life's mission.

Now the water before you is your child's Jordan. God the Father calls your little one his own, and the Holy Spirit enters your child's life as guide and friend.

Following his baptism, Jesus overcame the Evil One. He conquered death on the cross and rose in triumph to everlasting life. Your child will experience these mysteries too, and Christ will offer your child, as a member of his body, the Church, his way, his truth, and his life.

The Profession of Faith

Faith alone sees into these great mysteries. So as you come to the baptismal font you make a profession of faith and vow to fight against the Evil One. The credal statements you respond to are a form of the Apostles' Creed, the ancient Christian summary of faith. All the great Christian mysteries are contained in it:

— the creation of the world by God;
— the mission of Jesus his Son;
— the mysteries of redemption and life that he works through the Spirit.

This is the substance of the faith you are to communicate to your child and the faith that enables you to understand the mystery of baptism you celebrate.

Baptizing with Water

Standing by the water, with faith as your guide, you are called to the moment of creation when the Spirit of God hovered over the dark waters of chaos and brought forth creation, beautiful, ordered, and full of divine energy, as the Book of Genesis poetically recalls.

Your child, immersed in the baptismal waters, shares the blessing given by the Spirit to all creation.

However dark or chaotic this world becomes, the Spirit will bring peace and light to your son or daughter.

Immersed in the baptismal waters, your child shares in the victory won by the Israelites when they were freed from the slavery of Egypt and brought to freedom through the waters of the Red Sea. Like them God will bring your child to share a promised reward.

The baptismal waters, too, are a sign of the water that flowed from Christ's side as he hung on the Cross. They are a sign of the life Jesus came to give us all.

With the use of water symbolizing these blessings, your child is baptized:

"I baptize you in the name of the Father, and of the Son, and of the Holy Spirit."

Can you see what these great biblical symbols instruct you to do for the infant you carry in your arms? Help your child be at home in this world. Enable your dear one to find God in this created world, to trust life no matter how difficult it becomes, to believe in the creative power of God whose love rules the sun, the moon, and the other stars.

Help your child be free from any fear that would enslave, any false value or illusion that would enchain. Encourage your son or daughter to aim high.

Teach your child to know Jesus Christ. Knowing him is greater than anything else.

The Anointing, the White Garment and the Lighted Candle

The baptismal ceremony adds other signs that speak of the mysterious gift God makes to your child through Jesus Christ. Your son or daughter is anointed with oil. Like Christ who was anointed Priest, Prophet, and King, your child is called to worship and proclaim God's truth and is charged with caring for life and creation.

A white garment is given for your child to wear, a symbol of the dignity and purity that one who belongs to Christ possesses.

A candle, lighted from the Easter candle, is presented to the child, a sign of enlightenment by Christ. Held by the parent or godparent, its light is a reminder that Christ will continue to enlighten this child who is his own.

How precious in the sight of God is the little child you hold in your arms!

Concluding Ceremony: The Lord's Prayer and Final Blessing

After the baptism, you will bring your child to the altar where all pray the Our Father, the great prayer Jesus taught us to say as children of God. It is a model for teaching your child how to pray.

Finally the celebrant blesses the mother, the father, and then all those participating in the baptism. It is a blessing God always extends to those who bring new life into the world and care for children. Blessed by God you go forth to raise a child of God.

RITE OF BAPTISM FOR SEVERAL CHILDREN

RECEPTION OF THE CHILDREN

STAND

If possible, baptism should take place on Sunday, the day on which the Church celebrates the paschal mystery. It should be conferred in a communal celebration for all the recently born children, and in the presence of the faithful, or at least of relatives, friends, and neighbors, who are all to take an active part in the rite.

It is the role of the father and mother, accompanied by the godparents, to present the child to the Church for baptism.

If there are very many children, and if there are several priests or deacons present, these may help the celebrant in the parts referred to below.

The rite begins at the entrance to the church. The people may sing a psalm or hymn suitable for the occasion. (See pp. 57-64.)

Dialogue with Parents and Godparents

The celebrant greets all present and then questions the parents, using these or similar words:

Celebrant: What name do you give your child? (*or:* have you given?)

Parents: N.

Celebrant: What do you ask of God's Church for N.?

Parents: **Baptism.**

In the second response the parents may use other words, e.g., "faith," "the grace of Christ," "entrance into the Church," "eternal life."

If there are many children to be baptized, the celebrant asks the names from all the parents together, and each family replies in turn. The second question may also be asked of all together.

Celebrant: What name do you give each of these children? (*or:* have you given?)

Parents: N., N., etc.

Celebrant: What do you ask of God's Church for your children?

All: **Baptism.**

The celebrant then speaks to the parents in these or similar words:

You have asked to have your children baptized. In doing so you are accepting the responsibility of training them in the practice of the faith. It will be your duty to bring them up to keep God's commandments as Christ taught us, by loving God and our neighbor. Do you clearly understand what you are undertaking?

Parents: **We do.**

This response is given by each family individually. But if there are many children to be baptized, the response may be given by all together.

Then the celebrant turns to the godparents and addresses them in these or similar words:

Are you ready to help these parents in their duty as Christian mothers and fathers?

All the godparents: **We are.**

Signing the Forehead of the Children

The celebrant continues:

N. and N. (*or,* My dear children), the Christian community welcomes you with great joy. In its name I claim you for Christ our Savior by the sign of his cross. I now trace the cross on your foreheads, and invite your parents (and godparents) to do the same.

He signs each child on the forehead, in silence. Then he invites the parents and the godparents to do the same.

The celebrant invites the parents, godparents, and the others to take part in the liturgy of the word. If circumstances permit, there is a procession to the place where this will be celebrated, during which a song is sung, e.g.:

Song

We Come to You, Lord Jesus

VENIAMUS, DOMINE Irregular

(𝅗𝅥 = 58)
F Eb F Cm7 F Eb F Cm7
f Cantor: All repeat as needed
We come to you, Lord Je - sus.
Fill us with your life, make us chil-dren of the Fa-ther, and
F Eb F Cm7
Fmaj7 Bb Bbm Fmaj7 C Fmaj7
ending
one in — you. (We)

TEXT: From the *Rite of Baptism for Children* © 1969, International Committee on English in the Liturgy, Inc. (ICEL). All rights reserved.
TUNE: Ralph Verdi, C.PP.S. from *Music for Rite of Funerals and of Baptism for Children* © 1977, ICEL, Inc. All rights reserved.

The children to be baptized may be carried to a separate place, where they remain until the end of the liturgy of the word.

LITURGY OF THE WORD

Scriptural Readings **SIT**

One or more Scripture readings are proclaimed, during which all may sit if convenient.

Between the readings, a responsorial psalm may be sung.

Homily

After the reading, the celebrant gives a short homily, explaining to those present the significance of what has been read.

After the homily there may be a period of silence. If convenient, a suitable song follows. (See pp. 57-64.)

Intercessions (Prayer of the Faithful) **STAND**

Then the prayer of the faithful is said. The following or other intercessions may be used.

Celebrant: My brothers and sisters, let us ask our Lord Jesus Christ to look lovingly on these children who are to be baptized, on their parents and godparents, and on all the baptized.

Leader: By the mystery of your death and resurrection, bathe these children in light, give them the new life of baptism and welcome them into your holy Church.

All: **Lord, hear our prayer.**

Leader: Through baptism and confirmation, make them your faithful followers and witnesses to your gospel.

All: **Lord, hear our prayer.**

Leader: Lead them by a holy life to the joys of God's kingdom.

All: **Lord, hear our prayer.**

Leader: Make the lives of their parents and godparents examples of faith to inspire these children.

All: **Lord, hear our prayer.**

Leader: Keep their families always in your love.

All: **Lord, hear our prayer.**

Leader: Renew the grace of our baptism in each one of us.

All: **Lord, hear our prayer.**

Invocation of the Saints

The celebrant next invites all present to invoke the saints. At this point, if the children have been taken out, they are brought back.

Holy Mary, Mother of God, **pray for us.**
Saint John the Baptist, **pray for us.**
Saint Joseph, **pray for us.**
Saint Peter and Saint Paul, **pray for us.**

The names of other saints may be added, especially the patrons of the children to be baptized, and of the church or locality. The litany concludes:

All holy men and women, **pray for us.**

Prayer of Exorcism and Anointing before Baptism

After the invocations, the celebrant says one of the following:

A

Almighty and ever-living God,
you sent your only Son into the world
to cast out the power of Satan, spirit of evil,
to rescue man from the kingdom of darkness,
and bring him into the splendor of your kingdom of light.
We pray for these children:
set them free from original sin,
make them temples of your glory,
and send your Holy Spirit to dwell within them.

We ask this through Christ our Lord.

All: **Amen.**

B

Almighty God,
you sent your only Son
to rescue us from the slavery of sin,
and to give us the freedom
only your sons and daughters enjoy.

We now pray for these children
who will have to face the world with its temptations,
and fight the devil in all his cunning.

Your Son died and rose again to save us.
By his victory over sin and death,

cleanse these children from the stain of original sin.
Strengthen them with the grace of Christ,
and watch over them at every step in life's journey.

We ask this through Christ our Lord.

All: **Amen.**

The celebrant continues:

We anoint you with the oil of salvation
in the name of Christ our Savior;
may he strengthen you
with his power,
who lives and reigns for ever and ever.

All: **Amen.**

He anoints each child on the breast with the oil of catechumens. If the number of children is large, the anointing may be done by several ministers.

The anointing before baptism may be omitted if the celebrant judges the omission to be pastorally necessary or desirable. In that case he says once only:

May you have strength in the power of Christ our Savior, who lives and reigns for ever and ever.

All: **Amen.**

And immediately he lays his hand on each child in silence.

Then they go to the place where the baptism will take place.

Meanwhile, if it can be done suitably, an appropriate song is sung.

Song

Psalm 23:1-3, 4, 5, 6

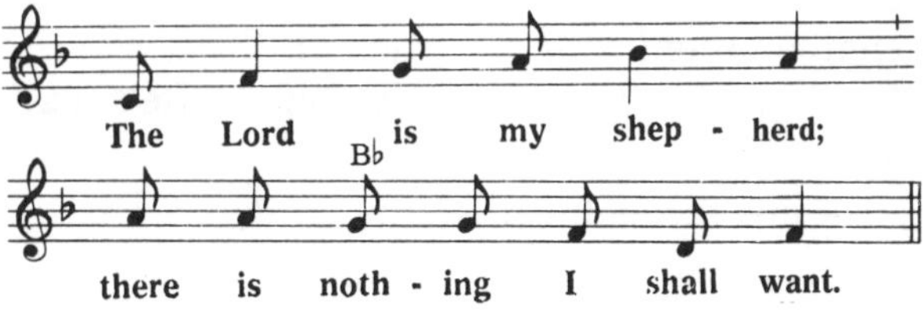
The Lord is my shep - herd;
B♭
there is noth - ing I shall want.

The Lord is my shepherd; I shall not want.
In verdant pastures he gives me repose;
Beside restful waters he leads me;
he refreshes my soul.
He guides me in right paths
for his name's sake.— ℟.

Even though I walk in the dark valley
I fear no evil; for you are at my side
With your rod and your staff
that give me courage.— ℟.

You spread the table before me
in the sight of my foes;
You anoint my head with oil;
my cup overflows.-- ℟.

Only goodness and kindness follow me
all the days of my life;
And I shall dwell in the house of the Lord
for years to come.— ℟.

CELEBRATION OF THE SACRAMENT

When they come to the font, the celebrant briefly reminds the congregation of the wonderful work of God whose plan it is to sanctify man, body and soul, through water. He may use these or similar words:

A

My dear brothers and sisters, we now ask God to give these children new life in abundance through water and the Holy Spirit.

B

My dear brothers and sisters, God uses the sacrament of water to give his divine life to those who believe in him. Let us turn to him, and ask him to pour his gift of life from this font on the children he has chosen.

Blessing and Invocation of God over Baptismal Water

Then, turning to the font, he says one of the following blessings:

A

Father, you give us grace through sacramental signs, which tell us of the wonders of your unseen power.

In baptism we use your gift of water, which you have made a rich symbol of the grace you give us in this sacrament.

At the very dawn of creation your Spirit breathed on the waters, making them the wellspring of all holiness.

The waters of the great flood you made a sign of the waters of baptism, that make an end of sin and a new beginning of goodness.

Through the waters of the Red Sea you led Israel out of slavery, to be an image of God's holy people, set free from sin by baptism.

In the waters of the Jordan your Son was baptized by John and anointed with the Spirit.

Your Son willed that water and blood should flow from his side as he hung upon the cross.

After his resurrection he told his disciples: "Go out and teach all nations, baptizing them in the name of the Father, and of the Son, and of the Holy Spirit."

Father, look now with love upon your Church, and unseal for her the fountain of baptism.

By the power of the Spirit give to the water of this font the grace of your Son.

You created man in your own likeness: cleanse him from sin in a new birth to innocence by water and the Spirit.

The celebrant touches the water with his right hand and continues:

We ask you, Father, with your Son to send the Holy Spirit upon the water of this font. May all who are buried with Christ in the death of baptism rise also with him to newness of life. We ask this through Christ our Lord.

All: **Amen.**

B

Celebrant: Praise to you, almighty God and Father, for you have created water to cleanse and to give life.

All: **Blessed be God** *(or some other suitable acclamation by the people).*

Celebrant: Praise to you, Lord Jesus Christ, the Father's only Son, for you offered yourself on the cross, that in the blood and water flowing from your side, and through your death and resurrection, the Church might be born.

All: **Blessed be God.**

Celebrant: Praise to you, God the Holy Spirit, for you anointed Christ at his baptism in the waters of Jordan, so that we might all be baptized into you.

All: **Blessed be God.**

The following invocations are said only if the baptismal water has not been blessed:

Celebrant: Come to us, Lord, Father of all, and make holy this water which you have created, so that all who are baptized in it may be washed clean of sin, and be born again to live as your children.

All: **Hear us, Lord** *(or some other suitable invocation).*

Celebrant: Make this water holy, Lord, so that all who are baptized into Christ's death and resurrection by this water may become more perfectly like your Son.

All: **Hear us, Lord.**

The celebrant touches the water with his right hand and continues:

Lord, make holy this water which you have created, so that all those whom you have chosen may be born again by the power of the Holy Spirit, and may take their place among your holy people.

All: **Hear us, Lord.**

You have called your children, N., N., to this cleansing water that they may share in the faith of your Church and have eternal life. By the mystery of this consecrated water lead them to a new and spiritual birth. We ask this through Christ our Lord.

All: **Amen**

C

Celebrant: Father, God of mercy, through these waters of baptism you have filled us with new life as your very own children.

All: **Blessed be God** *(or some other suitable acclamation by the people).*

Celebrant: From all who are baptized in water and the Holy Spirit, you have formed one people, united in your Son Jesus Christ.

All: **Blessed be God.**

Celebrant: You have set us free and filled our hearts with the Spirit of your love, that we may live in your peace.

All: **Blessed be God.**

Celebrant: You call those who have been baptized to announce the Good News of Jesus Christ to people everywhere.

All: **Blessed be God.**

If the baptismal water has not been blessed, the celebrant says:

Celebrant: You have called your children, N., N., to this cleansing water and new birth that by sharing the faith of your Church they might have eternal life. Bless ✠ this water in which they will be baptized. We ask this in the name of Christ our Lord.

All: **Amen.**

If the baptismal water has already been blessed, the celebrant omits the last prayer and says:

Celebrant: You have called your children, N., N., to this cleansing water that they may share in the faith of your Church and have eternal life. By the mystery of this consecrated water lead them to a new and spiritual birth. We ask this through Christ our Lord.

All: **Amen.**

Renunciation of Sin

The celebrant speaks to the parents and godparents in these words:

Dear parents and godparents: You have come here to present these children for baptism. By water and the Holy Spirit they are to receive the gift of new life from God, who is love.

On your part, you must make it your constant care to bring them up in the practice of the faith. See that the divine life which God gives them is kept safe from the poison of sin, to grow always stronger in their hearts.

If your faith makes you ready to accept this responsibility, renew now the vows of your own baptism. Reject sin; profess your faith in Christ Jesus. This is the faith of the Church. This is the faith in which these children are about to be baptized.

The celebrant questions the parents and godparents, using one of the following forms:

A

Celebrant: Do you reject Satan?

Parents and godparents: **I do.**

Celebrant: And all his works?

Parents and godparents: **I do.**

Celebrant: And all his empty promises?

Parents and godparents: **I do.**

B

Celebrant: Do you reject sin, so as to live in the freedom of God's children:

Parents and godparents: **I do.**

Celebrant: Do you reject the glamor of evil, and refuse to be mastered by sin?

Parents and godparents: **I do.**

Celebrant: Do you reject Satan, father of sin and prince of darkness?

Parents and godparents: **I do.**

Profession of Faith

Next the celebrant asks for the threefold profession of faith from the parents and godparents:

Celebrant: Do you believe in God, the Father almighty, creator of heaven and earth?

Parents and godparents: **I do.**

Celebrant: Do you believe in Jesus Christ, his only Son, our Lord, who was born of the Virgin Mary, was crucified, died, and was buried, rose from the dead, and is now seated at the right hand of the Father?

Parents and godparents: **I do.**

Celebrant: Do you believe in the Holy Spirit, the holy catholic Church, the communion of saints, the forgiveness of sins, the resurrection of the body, and life everlasting?

Parents and godparents: **I do.**

The celebrant and the congregation give their assent to this profession of faith:

Celebrant: This is our faith. This is the faith of the Church. We are proud to profess it, in Christ Jesus our Lord.

All: **Amen.**

Baptism

The celebrant invites the first of the families to the font. Using the name of the individual child, he questions the parents and godparents.

Celebrant: **Is it your will that** N. **should be baptized in the faith of the Church, which we have all professed with you?**

Parents and godparents: **It is.**

He baptizes the child, saying:

N., **I baptize you in the name of the Father,**

He immerses the child or pours water upon it.

and of the Son,

He immerses the child or pours water upon it a second time:

and of the Holy Spirit.

He immerses the child or pours water upon it a third time.

He asks the same question and performs the same action for each child.

After each baptism it is appropriate for the people to sing a short acclamation.

Smoothly (♩ = c. 72) Christopher Willcock, S.J.

All of you are one: u - ni - ted in Christ Je - sus;
all of you are one: u - ni - ted in Christ Je - sus.

or:

Arthur Hutchings

Bles - sed be God who chose— you in Christ.

If the baptism is performed by the pouring of water, it is preferable that the child be held by the mother or father. If baptism is by immersion, the mother or father lifts the child out of the font.

EXPLANATORY RITES

Anointing after Baptism

Then the celebrant says:

God the Father of our Lord Jesus Christ has freed you from sin, given you a new birth by water and the Holy Spirit, and welcomed you into his holy people. He now anoints you with the chrism of salvation. As Christ was anointed Priest, Prophet, and King, so may you live always as members of his body, sharing everlasting life.

All: **Amen.**

Next, the celebrant anoints each child on the crown of the head with chrism, in silence.

Clothing with White Garment

The celebrant says:

(N., N.,) you have become a new creation, and have clothed yourselves in Christ. See in this white garment the outward sign of our Christian dignity. With your family and friends to help you by word and example, bring that dignity unstained into the everlasting life of heaven.

All: **Amen.**

The white garments are put on the children. It is desirable that the families provide the garments.

Lighted Candle

The celebrant takes the Easter candle and says:

Receive the light of Christ.

Someone from each family (e.g., the father or godfather) lights the child's candle from the Easter candle.

The celebrant then says:

Parents and godparents, this light is entrusted to you to be kept burning brightly. These children of yours have been enlightened by Christ. They are to walk always as children of the light. May they keep the flame of faith alive in their hearts. When the Lord comes, may they go out to meet him with all the saints in the heavenly kingdom.

Ephphetha or Prayer over Ears and Mouth

The rite of Ephphetha may be performed at the discretion of the celebrant. He touches the ears and mouth of each child with his thumb, saying:

The Lord Jesus made the deaf hear and the dumb speak. May he soon touch your ears to receive his word, and your mouth to proclaim his faith, to the praise and glory of God the Father.

All: **Amen.**

CONCLUSION OF THE RITE

Next there is a procession to the altar, unless the baptism was performed in the sanctuary. The lighted candles are carried for the children.

A baptismal song is appropriate at this time, e.g.:

Song

You Have Put on Christ

BAPTIZED IN CHRIST Irregular

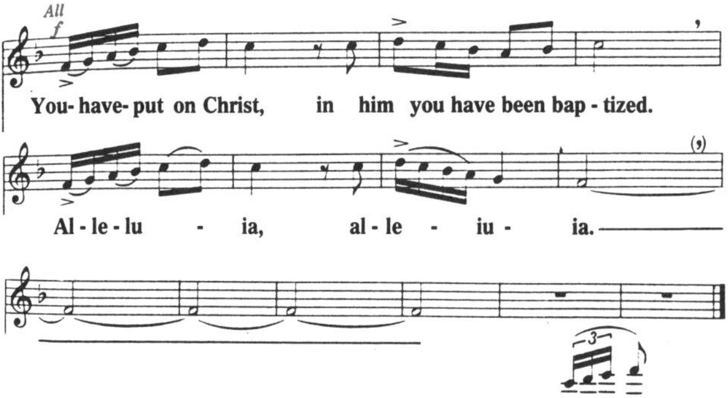
All
f
You- have- put on Christ, in him you have been bap - tized.
Al - le - lu - ia, al - le - lu - ia.

Other songs may be chosen (see pp. 57-64).

Lord's Prayer

The celebrant stands in front of the altar and addresses the parents, godparents, and the whole assembly in these or similar words:

Dearly beloved, these children have been reborn in baptism. They are now called children of God, for so indeed they are. In confirmation they will receive the fullness of God's Spirit. In holy communion they will share the banquet of Christ's sacrifice, calling God their Father in the midst of the Church. In their name, in the Spirit of our common sonship, let us pray together in the words our Lord has given us:

All present join the celebrant in singing or saying:

Our Father, who art in heaven,
hallowed be thy name;
thy kingdom come;
thy will be done on earth as it is in heaven.
Give us this day our daily bread;
and forgive us our trespasses
as we forgive those who trespass against us;
and lead us not into temptation,
but deliver us from evil.

Blessing and Dismissal

The celebrant first blesses the mothers, who hold the children in their arms, then the fathers, and lastly the entire assembly. All respond Amen to each prayer of blessing.

Celebrant: Go in peace.

All: **Thanks be to God.**

After the blessing, all may sing a hymn which suitably expresses thanksgiving and Easter joy, or they may sing the song of the Blessed Virgin Mary, the Magnificat. (See pp. 57-64.)

RITE OF BAPTISM FOR ONE CHILD

RECEPTION OF THE CHILD

STAND

If possible, baptism should take place on Sunday, the day on which the Church celebrates the paschal mystery. It should be conferred in a communal celebration in the presence of the faithful, or at least of relatives, friends, and neighbors, who are all to take an active part in the rite.

It is the role of the father and mother, accompanied by the godparents, to present the child to the Church for baptism.

The rite begins at the entrance to the church. The people may sing a psalm or hymn suitable for the occasion. (See pp. **57-64.**)

Dialogue with Parents and Godparents

The celebrant greets all present and then questions the parents, using these or similar words:

Celebrant: What name do you give your child? (*or:* have you given?)

Parents: **N.**

Celebrant: What do you ask of God's Church for N.?

Parents: **Baptism**

In the second response the parents may use other words, such as, "faith," "the grace of Christ," "entrance into the Church," "eternal life."

The celebrant then speaks to the parents in these or similar words:

You have asked to have your child baptized. In doing so you are accepting the responsibility of training him/her in the practice of the faith. It will be your duty to bring him/her up to keep God's commandments as Christ taught us, by loving God and our neighbor. Do you clearly understand what you are undertaking?

Parents: **We do.**

Then the celebrant turns to the godparents and addresses them in these or similar words:

Are you ready to help the parents of this child in their duty as Christian parents?

Godparents: **We are.**

Signing the Forehead of the Child

The celebrant continues:

N., the Christian community welcomes you with great joy. In its name I claim you for Christ our

Savior by the sign of his cross. I now trace the cross on your forehead, and invite your parents (and godparents) to do the same.

He signs the child on the forehead, in silence. Then he invites the parents and the godparents to do the same.

The celebrant invites the parents, godparents, and the others to take part in the liturgy of the word. If circumstances permit, there is a procession to the place where this will be celebrated, during which a song is sung, e.g.:

Song — We Come to You, Lord Jesus

VENIAMUS, DOMINE Irregular

(♩=58)
F Eb F Cm7 F Eb F Cm7
f Cantor: All repeat as needed
We come to you, Lord Je - sus.
Fill us with your life, make us chil-dren of the Fa-ther, and
F Eb F Cm7
Fmaj7 Bb Bbm Fmaj7 C Fmaj7
ending
one in— you. (We)

TEXT: From the *Rite of Baptism for Children* © 1969, International Committee on English in the Liturgy, Inc. (ICEL). All rights reserved.
TUNE: Ralph Verdi, C.PP.S. from *Music for Rite of Funerals and of Baptism for Children* © 1977, ICEL, Inc. All rights reserved.

LITURGY OF THE WORD

Scriptural Readings

SIT

One or more Scripture readings are proclaimed, during which all may sit if convenient.

Between the readings, responsorial psalms or verses may be sung.

Homily

After the reading, the celebrant gives a short homily, explaining to those present the significance of what has been read.

After the homily there may be a period of silence. If convenient, a suitable song follows. (See pp. **57-64.**)

Intercessions (Prayer of the Faithful)

STAND

Then the prayer of the faithful is said. The following or other intercessions may be used.

Celebrant: My dear brothers and sisters, let us ask our Lord Jesus Christ to look lovingly on this child who is to be baptized, on his/her parents and godparents, and on all the baptized.

Leader: By the mystery of your death and resurrection, bathe this child in light, give him/her into your new life of baptism and welcome him/her into your holy Church.

All: **Lord, hear our prayer.**

Leader: Through baptism and confirmation, make him/her your faithful follower and a witness to your gospel.

All: **Lord, hear our prayer.**

Leader: Lead him/her by a holy life to the joys of God's kingdom.

All: **Lord, hear our prayer.**

Leader: Make the lives of his/her parents and godparents examples of faith to inspire this child.

All: **Lord, hear our prayer.**

Leader: Keep his/her family always in your love.

All: **Lord, hear our prayer.**

Leader: Renew the grace of our baptism in each one of us.

All: **Lord, hear our prayer.**

Invocation of the Saints

The celebrant next invites all present to invoke the saints.

Holy Mary, Mother of God,	**pray for us.**
St. John the Baptist,	**pray for us.**
Saint Joseph,	**pray for us.**
Saint Peter and Saint Paul,	**pray for us.**

The names of other saints may be added, especially the patrons of the child to be baptized, and of the church or locality. The litany concludes:

All holy men and women,	**pray for us.**

Prayer of Exorcism and Anointing before Baptism

After the invocation, the celebrant says one of the following:

A

Almighty and ever-living God,
you sent your only Son into the world

to cast out the power of Satan, spirit of evil,
to rescue man from the kingdom of darkness,
and bring him into the splendor of your kingdom of light.
We pray for this child:
set him/her free from original sin,
make him/her a temple of your glory,
and send your Holy Spirit to dwell with him/her.

We ask this through Christ our Lord.

All: **Amen.**

B

Almighty God,
you sent your only Son
to rescue us from the slavery of sin,
and to give us the freedom
only your sons and daughters enjoy.

We now pray for this child
who will have to face the world with its temptations,
and fight the devil in all his cunning.

Your Son died and rose again to save us.
By his victory over sin and death,
cleanse this child from the stain of original sin.

Strengthen him/her with the grace of Christ,
and watch over him/her at every step in life's journey.

We ask this through Christ our Lord.

All: **Amen.**

The celebrant continues:

We anoint you with the oil of salvation
in the name of Christ our Savior;
may he strengthen you
with his power,
who lives and reigns for ever and ever.

All: **Amen.**

He anoints the child on the breast with the oil of catechumens.

The anointing before baptism may be omitted if the minister of baptism judges the omission to be pastorally necessary or desirable. In that case he says:

May you have strength in the power of Christ our Savior, who lives and reigns for ever and ever.

All: **Amen.**

And immediately he lays his hand on the child in silence.

Then they go to the place where the baptism will take place.

CELEBRATION OF THE SACRAMENT

When they come to the font, the celebrant briefly reminds the congregation of the wonderful work of God whose plan it is to sanctify man, body and soul, through water. He may use these or similar words:

A

My dear brothers and sisters, we now ask God to give this child new life in abundance through water and the Holy Spirit.

B

My dear brothers and sisters, God uses the sacrament of water to give his divine life to those who believe in him. Let us turn to him, and ask him to pour his gift of life from this font on this child he has chosen.

Blessing and Invocation of God over Baptismal Water

Then, turning to the font, he says one of the following blessings:

A

Father, you give us grace through sacramental signs, which tell us of the wonders of your unseen power.

In baptism we use your gift of water, which you have made a rich symbol of the grace you give us in this sacrament.

At the very dawn of creation your Spirit breathed on the waters, making them the wellspring of all holiness.

The waters of the great flood you made a sign of the waters of baptism, that make an end of sin and a new beginning of goodness.

Through the waters of the Red Sea you led Israel out of slavery, to be an image of God's holy people, set free from sin by baptism.

In the waters of the Jordan your Son was baptized by John and anointed with the Spirit.

Your Son willed that water and blood should flow from his side as he hung upon the cross.

After his resurrection he told his disciples: "Go out and teach all nations, baptizing them in the name of the Father, and of the Son, and of the Holy Spirit."

Father, look now with love upon your Church, and unseal for her the fountain of baptism.

By the power of the Spirit give to the water of this font the grace of your Son.

You created man in your likeness: cleanse him from sin in a new birth to innocence by water and the Spirit.

The celebrant touches the water with his right hand and continues:

We ask you, Father, with your Son to send the Holy Spirit upon the water of this font. May all who are buried with Christ in the death of baptism rise also with him to newness of life. We ask this through Christ our Lord.

All: **Amen.**

B

Celebrant: Praise to you, almighty God and Father, for you have created water to cleanse and to give life.

All: **Blessed be God** (*or some other suitable acclamation by the people*).

Celebrant: Praise to you, Lord Jesus Christ, the Father's only Son, for you offered yourself on the cross, that in the blood and water flowing from your side, and through your death and resurrection, the Church might be born.

All: **Blessed be God.**

Celebrant: Praise to you, God the Holy Spirit, for you anointed Christ at his baptism in the waters of Jordan, so that we might all be baptized into you.

All: **Blessed be God.**

The following invocations are said only if the baptismal water has not been blessed:

Celebrant: Come to us, Lord, Father of all, and make holy this water which you have created, so that all who are baptized in it may be washed clean of sin, and be born again to live as your children.

All: **Hear us, Lord** (*or some other suitable invocation*).

Celebrant: Make this water holy, Lord, so that all who are baptized into Christ's death and resurrection by this water may become more perfectly like your Son.

All: **Hear us, Lord.**

The celebrant touches the water with his right hand and continues:

Lord, make holy this water which you have created, so that all those whom you have chosen may be born again by the power of the Holy Spirit, and may take their place among your holy people.

All: **Hear us, Lord.**

You have called your child, N., to this cleansing water that he/she may share in the faith of your Church and have eternal life. By the mystery of this consecrated water lead him/her to a new and spiritual birth. We ask this through Christ our Lord.

All: **Amen.**

C

Celebrant: Father, God of mercy, through these waters of baptism you have filled us with new life as your very own children.

All: **Blessed be God** (*or some other suitable acclamation by the people*).

Celebrant: From all who are baptized in water and the Holy Spirit, you have formed one people, united in your Son Jesus Christ.

All: **Blessed be God.**

Celebrant: You have set us free and filled our hearts with the Spirit of your love, that we may live in your peace.

All: **Blessed be God.**

Celebrant: You call those who have been baptized to announce the Good News of Jesus Christ to people everywhere.

All: **Blessed be God.**

If the baptismal water has not been blessed, the celebrant says:

Celebrant: You have called your child, N., to this cleansing water and new birth that by sharing the faith of your Church he/she might have eternal life. Bless ✠ this water in which he/she will be baptized. We ask this in the name of Christ our Lord.

All: **Amen.**

If the baptismal water has already been blessed, the celebrant omits the last prayer and says:

Celebrant: You have called your child N., to this cleansing water that he/she may share in the faith of your Church and have eternal life. By the mystery of this consecrated water lead him/her to a new and spiritual birth. We ask this through Christ our Lord.

All: **Amen.**

Renunciation of Sin

The celebrant speaks to the parents and godparents in these words:

Dear parents and godparents: You have come here to present this child for baptism. By water and the Holy Spirit he/she is to receive the gift of new life from God, who is love.

On your part, you must make it your constant care to bring him/her up in the practice of the faith. See that the divine life which God gives him/her is kept safe from the poison of sin, to grow always stronger in his/her heart.

If your faith makes you ready to accept this responsibility, renew now the vows of your own baptism. Reject sin; profess your faith in Christ Jesus. This is the faith of the Church. This is the faith in which this child is about to be baptized.

The celebrant questions the parents and godparents, using one of the following forms:

A

Celebrant: Do you reject Satan?
Parents and godparents: **I do.**
Celebrant: And all his works?
Parents and godparents: **I do.**
Celebrant: And all his empty promises?
Parents and godparents: **I do.**

B

Celebrant: Do you reject sin, so as to live in the freedom of God's children:
Parents and godparents: **I do.**

Celebrant: Do you reject the glamor of evil, and refuse to be mastered by sin?

Parents and godparents: **I do.**

Celebrant: Do you reject Satan, father of sin and prince of darkness?

Parents and godparents: **I do.**

Profession of Faith

Next the celebrant asks for the threefold profession of faith from the parents and godparents:

Celebrant: Do you believe in God, the Father almighty, creator of heaven and earth?

Parents and godparents: **I do.**

Celebrant: Do you believe in Jesus Christ, his only Son, our Lord, who was born of the Virgin Mary, was crucified, died, and was buried, rose from the dead, and is now seated at the right hand of the Father?

Parents and godparents: **I do.**

Celebrant: Do you believe in the Holy Spirit, the holy catholic Church, the communion of saints, the forgiveness of sins, the resurrection of the body, and life everlasting?

Parents and godparents: **I do.**

The celebrant and the congregation give their assent to this profession of faith:

Celebrant: This is our faith. This is the faith of the Church. We are proud to profess it, in Christ Jesus our Lord.

All: **Amen.**

Baptism

The celebrant invites the family to the font. Using the name of the child, he questions the parents and godparents.

Celebrant: **Is it your will that** N. **should be baptized in the faith of the Church, which we have all professed with you?**

Parents and godparents: **It is.**

He baptizes the child, saying:

N., **I baptize you in the name of the Father,**

He immerses the child or pours water upon it.

and of the Son,

He immerses the child or pours water upon it a second time:

and the Holy Spirit.

He immerses the child or pours water upon it a third time.

After the child is baptized, it is appropriate for the people to sing a short acclamation:

Smoothly (♩ = c. 72) Christopher Willcock, S.J.

All of you are one: u - ni - ted in Christ Je - sus;
all of you are one: u - ni - ted in Christ Je - sus.

TEXT: From the *Rite of Baptism for Children* © 1969, International Committee on English in the Liturgy, Inc. (ICEL). All rights reserved.
MUSIC: From *Music for the Rites: Baptism, Eucharist, and Ordinations* © 1978, ICEL, Inc. All rights reserved.

or:

Arthur Hutchings

Bles - sed be God who chose— you in Christ.

If the baptism is performed by the pouring of water, it is preferable that the child be held by the mother or father. If baptism is by immersion, the mother or father lifts the child out of the font.

EXPLANATORY RITES

Anointing after Baptism

Then the celebrant says:

God the Father of our Lord Jesus Christ has freed you from sin, given you a new birth by water and the Holy Spirit, and welcomed you into his holy people. He now anoints you with the chrism of salvation. As Christ was anointed Priest, Prophet, and King, so may you live always as a member of his body, sharing everlasting life.

All: **Amen.**

The celebrant anoints the child on the crown of the head with chrism, in silence.

Clothing with White Garment

The celebrant says:

N., you have become a new creation, and have clothed yourself in Christ. See in this white garment the outward sign of your Christian dignity.

With your family and friends to help you by word and example, bring that dignity unstained into the everlasting life of heaven.

All: **Amen.**

The white garment is put on the child. It is desirable that the family provide the garment.

Lighted Candle

The celebrant takes the Easter candle and says:

Receive the light of Christ.

Someone from the family (such as the father or godfather) lights the child's candle from the Easter candle.

The celebrant then says:

Parents and godparents, this light is entrusted to you to be kept burning brightly. This child of yours has been enlightened by Christ. He/she is to walk always as a child of the light. May he/she keep the flame of faith alive in his/her heart. When the Lord comes, may he/she go out to meet him with all the saints in the heavenly kingdom.

Ephphetha or Prayer over Ears and Mouth

The rite of Ephphetha may be performed at the discretion of the celebrant. He touches the ears and mouth of the child with his thumb, saying:

The Lord Jesus made the deaf hear and the dumb speak. May he soon touch your ears to receive his word, and your mouth to proclaim his faith, to the praise and glory of God the Father.

All: **Amen.**

CONCLUSION OF THE RITE

Next there is a procession to the altar, unless the baptism was performed in the sanctuary. The lighted candle is carried for the child.

A baptismal song is appropriate at this time, e.g.:

Song

You Have Put on Christ

BAPTIZED IN CHRIST Irregular

All
You- have- put on Christ, in him you have been bap - tized.
Al - le - lu - ia, al - le - iu - ia.

Other songs may be chosen (see pp. 57-64).

Lord's Prayer

The celebrant stands in front of the altar and addresses the parents, godparents, and the whole assembly in these or similar words:

Dearly beloved, this child has been reborn in baptism. He/she is now called the child of God, for so indeed he/she is. In confirmation he/she will receive the fullness of God's Spirit. In holy communion he/she will share the banquet of Christ's sacrifice, calling God his/her Father in the midst of the Church. In the name of this child, in the Spirit of our common sonship, let us pray together in the words our Lord has given us:

All present join the celebrant in singing or saying:

Our Father, who art in heaven,
hallowed be thy name;
thy kingdom come;
thy will be done on earth as it is in heaven.
Give us this day our daily bread;
and forgive us our trespasses
as we forgive those who trespass against us;
and lead us not into temptation,
but deliver us from evil.

Blessing and Dismissal

The celebrant first blesses the mother, who holds the child in her arms, then the father, and lastly the entire assembly. All respond Amen to each prayer of blessing.

Celebrant: Go in peace.

All: **Thanks be to God.**

After the blessing, all may sing a hymn which suitably expresses thanksgiving and Easter joy, or they may sing the song of the Blessed Virgin Mary, the Magnificat. (See pp. 57-64.)

YOUR CHILD'S BAPTISM: A PRECIOUS MEMORY

Baptism is a sacrament we should remember all our lives. Later your child will receive two other sacraments—Holy Eucharist and Confirmation—which, along with baptism, are "sacraments of initiation." They are great sacraments that initiate us into the Christian life.

Remembering the Day of Baptism

Help your child realize the importance of baptism as he or she grows up. You can do it in small but significant ways. For example, try to recall your child's baptism each year.

On your child's birthday, or baptismal day, make the baptismal candle and baptismal robe part of the celebration, as well as pictures taken at that time. Each year your child will be reminded of the important day when he or she was christened.

Your Child's Patron Saint

Introduce your child to the saint whose name he or she bears. Children love to hear the story of their patron saints, who become at baptism their friends and guides through life.

Most saints have a day in the year on which their feast is celebrated. Try celebrating your child's patron saint's feastday.

Handing On Your Faith

Long before your son or daughter understands the gospel stories read in church, tell your child these stories yourselves in simple words and with colorful pictures that can be easily understood. Make your home the nursery of your child's faith.

You traced the Cross on your little one's forehead in the baptismal ceremony. Teach your child early on to make the Sign of the Cross, a simple expressive prayer. The Our Father and Hail Mary are also prayers your child should know. They should be among the first words your child speaks.

Holy Water, a sacramental the Church has always associated with the baptismal water, is a good reminder of baptism and its meaning

Invite your child's godparents to continue to show their interest in their godchild as the years pass, especially when the other sacraments are to be received.

"Unless You Become Like Children"

Some parents today mistakenly neglect their children's religious upbringing, "Let them make up their own minds when they get older," they say.

Jesus, however, saw children as capable of a rich spiritual life from their earliest years; indeed he offered the spirituality of the child as an example for adults to imitate. "Unless you turn and become like children you will not enter the kingdom of heaven" (Mt 18:3).

Commenting on Jesus' words, St. Leo the Great, one of the early Popes, offered a description of a child's spirituality. He said it is characterized by:

— freedom from crippling anxieties,
— forgetfulness of injuries,
— sociability,
— wonder at all things.

As parents you can do nothing better than encourage these excellent qualities in your children.

Children Free from Fear

Help them be free from crippling anxieties. It comes naturally to good parents to provide their children with food, clothing, love, and attention in their growing years, for instinctively they know their child's early life should be as carefree as possible. By being cared for, children learn to trust in someone beyond themselves and to believe in the goodness of others.

Such care nourishes in children an abiding belief in the providence of God. They will be able to take on the responsibilities of adult life without being crippled by anxieties. By experiencing a parent's care, they know God will provide. How blessed are children who grow into adults preserving a childlike trust in their heavenly Father, who knows what they need!

Learning Forgiveness

A normal child has a wonderful ability to forget injuries. We marvel at the resilience of children, even in the worst situations.

By encouraging your child to handle the inevitable setbacks of life gracefully, to forgive others, and to forget hurts received, you help form someone who can go through life unhindered by resentment or self-pity.

Getting Along with Others

Children, too, are born naturally sociable. Only in later life come the racial and social prejudices that spoil their dealings with others. Teach your children that, as Christians, Christ wants them to be at home with others as brothers and sisters.

Encourage that natural sociability in your child so that he or she may deal with people of different backgrounds, ages, nationalities, or social classes with equality and respect.

Wonder, a Child's Gift

Finally, children are born with a sense of wonder. They are born curious, wide-eyed, eager to learn, ready to be delighted. As their guides, nourish this gift of wonder in your children, lest it be deadened by the sense of boredom and gloom that permeates so much of our society today. Above all, teach them to wonder before the mystery of God.

Not surprisingly, the gospel records Jesus' great love for children. "He embraced them and blessed them, placing his hands on them" (Mk 10:16). Through you, may he do the same for your children.

SOME NORMS FOR BAPTISM

1. Baptism, the door to life and to the kingdom of God, is the first sacrament of the New Law, which Christ offered to all, that they might have eternal life. He later entrusted this sacrament and the Gospel to his Church, when he told his apostles: “Go, make disciples of all nations, and baptize them in the name of the Father, and of the Son, and of the Holy Spirit” (Mt 28:19). Baptism is therefore, above all, the sacrament of that faith by which, enlightened by the grace of the Holy Spirit, we respond to the Gospel of Christ.

That is why the Church believes that it is its most basic and necessary duty to inspire all, catechumens, parents of children still to be baptized, and godparents, to that true and living faith by which they hold fast to Christ and enter into or confirm their commitment to the New Covenant. In order to enliven such faith, the Church prescribes the pastoral instruction of catechumens, the preparation of the children’s parents, the celebration of God’s word, and the profession of faith at the celebration of baptism.

2. The preparation for baptism and Christian instruction are both of vital concern to God’s people, the Church, which hands on and nourishes the faith received from the apostles. Through the ministry of the Church, adults are called to the Gospel by the Holy Spirit and infants are baptized in the faith of the Church and brought up in that

faith. Therefore . . . catechists and other laypersons should work with priests and deacons in the preparation for baptism.

In the actual celebration, the people of God (represented not only by the parents, godparents, and relatives, but also . . . by friends, neighbors, and some members of the local Church) should take an active part. Thus they will show their common faith and the shared joy with which the newly baptized are received into the community of the Church.

3. Godparents are to be present in order to represent both the expanded spiritual family of the one to be baptized and the role of the Church as a mother. As occasion offers, godparents help the parents so that children will come to profess the faith and live up to it.

4. Those designated as godparents must have received the three sacraments of initiation, baptism, confirmation, and eucharist, and be living a life consistent with faith and with the responsibility of a godparent.

5. In imminent danger of death and especially at the moment of death, when no priest or deacon is available, any member of the faithful, indeed anyone with the right intention, may and sometimes must administer baptism.

6. As far as possible, all recently born babies should be baptized at a common celebration on the same day. Except for a good reason, baptism should not be celebrated more than once on the same day in the same church.

Rite of Christian Initiation of Adults
General Instruction, nos. 3, 7, 8, 10, 16, 27

INDEX OF SCRIPTURE READINGS IN THE RITE

Old Testament Readings

Exodus 17:3-7
Exodus 36:24-28
Ezekiel 47:1-9, 12

New Testament Readings

Romans 6:3-5
Romans 8:28-32
1 Corinthians 12:12-13
Galatians 3:26-29
Ephesians 4:1-6
1 Peter 2:4-5, 9-10

Responsorial Psalms

Psalm 23:1-3, 3-4, 5, 6
Psalm 27:1, 4, 8-9, 13-14
Psalm 34:2-3, 6-7, 8-9, 14-15, 16-17, 18-19

Alleluia Verse

John 3:16; 8:12; 14:6
Ephesians 4:5-6
2 Timothy 1:10
1 Peter 2:9

Gospel Readings

Matthew 28:18-30
Mark 1:9-11
Mark 10:13-16
John 3:1-6

Christ Is Made the Sure Foundation 1

REGENT SQUARE 8.7.8.7.8.7

1. Christ is made the sure foun - da - tion, Christ the head and
2. All that ded - i - cat - ed cit - y, Dear - ly loved of
3. To this tem - ple where we call you Come, Al - might - y
4. Grant, we pray, to all your ser - vants What they ask of

1. cor - ner - stone, Cho - sen of the Lord, and pre-cious,
2. God on high, In ex - ult - ant ju - bi - la - tion
3. Lord, to - day; Come with all your lov - ing kind-ness,
4. you to gain, What they gain of you for ev - er

1. Bind - ing all the— Church in one, Ho - ly Zi - on's
2. Pours per - pet - ual— mel - o - dy, God the One in
3. Hear your peo - ple— as they pray, And your full - est
4. With the bless - ed— to re - tain, And here - af - ter

1. help for ev - er, And her con - fi - dence a - lone.
2. Three a - dor - ing In glad hymns e - ter - nal - ly.
3. ben - e - dic - tion Give to us, O Lord, this day.
4. in your glo - ry Ev - er - more with you to reign.

5. Praise and honor to the Father,
Praise and honor to the Son,
Praise and honor to the Spirit,
Ever Three and ever One,
One in might and one in glory,
While unending ages run.

TEXT: *Urbs beata Hierusalem [Angularis fundamentum]*, Latin, c. 6th century, tr. by John Mason Neale, 1818-1866, in his *Hymnal Noted*, 1852, alt.
TUNE: Henry Thomas Smart, 1815-1879, for the English Presbyterian volume, *Psalms and Hymns for Divine Worship*, 1867.

At the Lamb's High Feast We Sing 2

Melody: Salzburg 77.77.D

Music: Jakob Hintze, 1622-1702
Text: *Ad regias Agni dapes*
adapted by Geoffrey Laycock

Translator: Robert Campell, 1814-1868.

1. **At the Lamb's high feast we sing**
Praise to our victor'ous King.
He has washed us in the tide
Flowing from his opened side;
Praise we him whose love divine
Gives his sacred Blood for wine,
Gives his Body for the feast,
Christ the Victim, Christ the Priest.

2. **When the Paschal blood is poured,**
Death's dark Angel sheathes his sword;
Israel's hosts triumphant go
Through the wave that drowns the foe.
Christ the Lamb, whose Blood was shed,
Paschal victim, Paschal bread;
Let us with fervent love
Taste the Manna from above.

3. **Mighty victim from on high,**
Pow'rs of hell now vanquished lie;
Sin is conquered in the fight:
You have brought us life and light;
Your resplendent banners wave,
You have risen from the grave;
Christ has opened Paradise,
And in him all men shall rise.

4. **Easter triumph, Easter joy,**
Sin alone can this destroy;
Souls from sin and death set free
Glory in their liberty.
Hymns of glory, hymns of praise
Father, unto you we raise;
Risen Lord, for joy we sing:
Let our hymns through heaven ring.

How Glad I Was to Hear Them Say 3

St. Anne C.M. (O God, Our Help in Ages Past)
TEXT: Psalm 122 (121): based on *Scottish Psalter*, 1650, alt.
TUNE: Later form of melody (rhythm adapted), attr. to William Croft, 1678-1727 in *A Supplement to the New Version of the Psalms*, 1708.

1. **How glad I was to hear them say,**
Come with us to God's home.
Jerusalem, within your gates
Our joyful feet will come.

2. **Jerusalem! a city fair**
Securely built and strong,
Where all the tribes of God go up
To worship in his throng.

3. **Now, for my friends' and brethren's sake,**
Peace be in you, I'll say.
And for the house of God our Lord,
I'll seek your good each day.

You Are the Way 4

St. Anne C.M. (*O God, Our Help in Ages Past*)
TEXT: George Washington Doane, 1799-1859, in *Verses for 1851 in Commemoration of the 3rd Jubilee of S.P.G.*, alt.
TUNE: Later form of melody (rhythm adapted), attr. to William Croft, 1678-1727 in *A Supplement to the New Version of the Psalms*, 1708.

1. **You are the way; to you alone**
From sin and death we flee;
And all who would the Father seek
Must seek you faithfully.

2. **You are the truth; your word alone**
True wisdom can impart;
You only can inform the mind
And purify the heart.

3. **You are the life; the rending tomb**
Proclaims your conquering arm;
And those who put their trust in you
Not death nor hell shall harm.

4. **You are the way, the truth, the life;**
Grant us that way to know,
That truth to keep, that life to win,
Whose joys eternal flow.

For All the Saints 5

SINE NOMINE 10 10 10 with alleluia*

1. For all the saints, who from their labors rest,
Who thee by faith before the world confessed,
Thy name, O Jesus, be for ever blessed. Alleluia! Alleluia!

2. Thou wast their rock, their fortress and their might;
Thou, Lord, their captain in the well-fought fight;
Thou in the darkness drear their one true light. Alleluia! Alleluia!

3. Oh, may thy soldiers, faithful, true, and bold
Fight as the saints who nobly fought of old,
And win with them the victors' crown of gold. Alleluia! Alleluia!

4. Oh, blest communion! fellowship divine!
We feebly struggle, they in glory shine!
Yet all are one in thee, for all are thine! Alleluia! Alleluia!

TEXT: William Walsham How, 1823-1897, in *Hymn for a Saint's Day and Other Hymns by a Layman,* 1864.

*SUGGESTED TUNE: Ralph Vaughan Williams, 1872-1958, in the *English Hymnal,* 1906.

Canticle of Mary 6

Lk 1:46-55 S.M. Skelly, S.C., 1975.

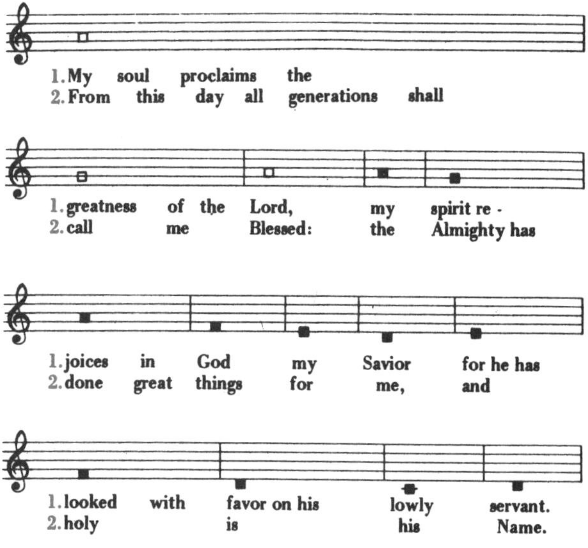
1. My soul proclaims the
2. From this day all generations shall
1. greatness of the Lord, my spirit re-
2. call me Blessed: the Almighty has
1. joices in God my Savior for he has
2. done great things for me, and
1. looked with favor on his lowly servant.
2. holy is his Name.

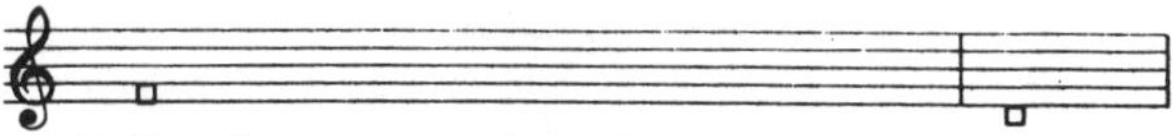

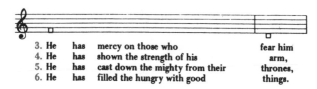

3. He has mercy on those who fear him
4. He has shown the strength of his arm,
5. He has cast down the mighty from their thrones,
6. He has filled the hungry with good things.

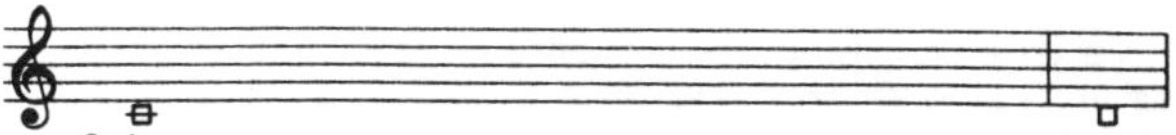

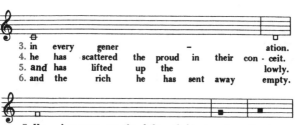

3. in every gener - ation.
4. he has scattered the proud in their con - ceit.
5. and has lifted up the lowly.
6. and the rich he has sent away empty.

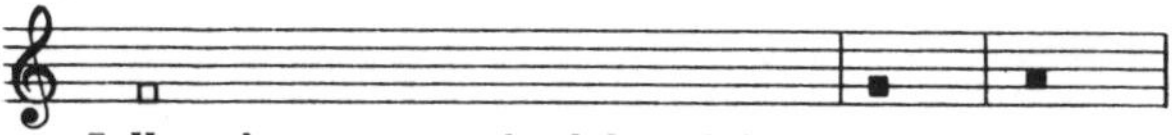

7. He has come to the help of his ser-vant Israel

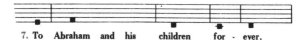

7. for he has re - membered his promise of mercy,
the promise he made to our fathers,

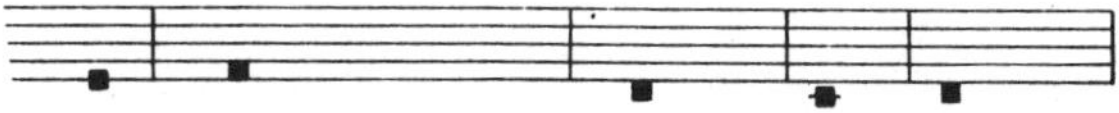

7. To Abraham and his children for - ever.

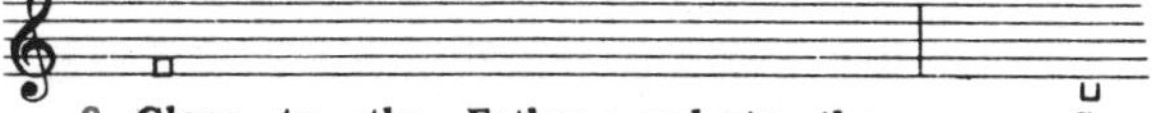

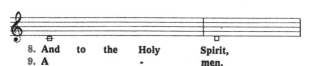

8. Glory to the Father, and to the Son,
9. As it was in the beginning, is now, and will be for ever,

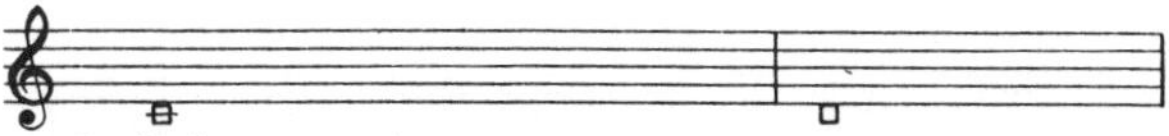

8. And to the Holy Spirit,
9. A - men.

Glory Be to God the Father 7

REGENT SQUARE 8.7.8.7.8.7*

1

Glory be to God the Father,
Glory be to God the Son,
Glory be to God the Spirit,
Glory to the Three in One!
Glory, honor, praise, and blessing,
While eternal ages run!

2

Glory be to him who loves us,
Washed us from each spot and stain!
Glory be to him who bought us,
Made us kings with him to reign!
Glory, honor, praise, and blessing
To the Lamb that once was slain!

3

Glory to the King of angels,
Glory to the Church's King,
Glory to the King of nations,
Heav'n and earth, your praises sing;
Glory, honor, praise, and blessing
To the King of glory bring!

St. Anne C.M. (*O God, Our Help in Ages Past*)
TEXT: Horarius Bonar, 1808-1899, in his *Hymns of Faith and Hope,* 3rd series, 1866, alt.
TUNE: Later form of melody (rhythm adapted), attr. to William Croft, 1678-1727 in *A Supplement to the New Version of the Psalms,* 1708.

Now Thank We All Our God 8

NUN DANKET 6.7.6.7.6.6.6.6

1

Now thank we all our God
With hearts and hands and voices,
Who wondrous things has done,
In whom the world rejoices;
Who, from our mothers' arms,
Has blest us on our way
With countless gifts of love,
And still is ours today.

2

O may this gracious God
Through all our life be near us,
With ever joyful hearts
And blessed peace to cheer us;
Preserve us in his grace,
And guide us in distress,
And free us from all sin,
Till heaven we possess.

3

All praise and thanks to God
The Father now be given,
The Son, and Spirit blest,
Who reigns in highest heaven,
Eternal, Triune God,
Whom earth and heav'n adore;
For thus it was, is now,
And shall be ever more.

TEXT: *Nun danket alle Gott,* Martin Rinkart, 1586-1649, in Johann Crüger's *Praxis Pietatis Melica,* 1647, tr. by Catherine Winkworth, 1827-1878, in her *Chorale-Book for England,* 1863, slightly alt.

TUNE: Later form of melody by Johann Crüger, 1598-1662, in his *Praxis Pietatis Melica,* 1647, harm. by Felix Mendelssohn-Bartholdy, 1809-1847, in his *Lobgesang,* opus 52, 1840.

I Sing the Mighty Power of God

9

ELLACOMBE C.M.D.

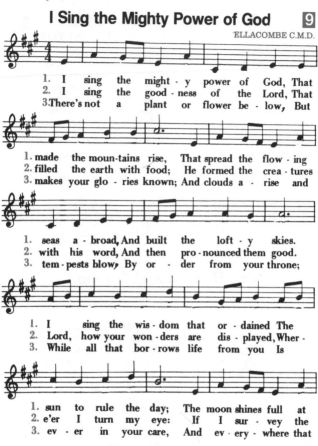

1. I sing the might - y power of God, That
2. I sing the good - ness of the Lord, That
3. There's not a plant or flower be - low, But

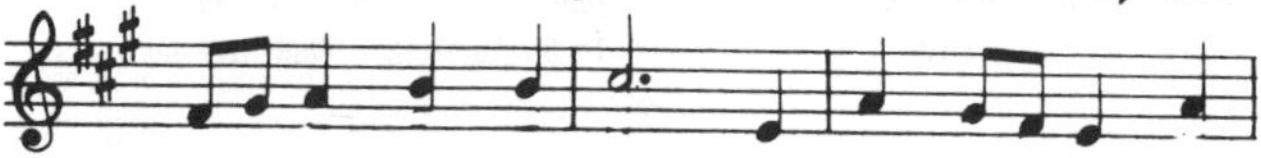

1. made the moun-tains rise, That spread the flow - ing
2. filled the earth with food; He formed the crea - tures
3. makes your glo - ries known; And clouds a - rise and

1. seas a - broad, And built the loft - y skies.
2. with his word, And then pro - nounced them good.
3. tem - pests blow, By or - der from your throne;

1. I sing the wis - dom that or - dained The
2. Lord, how your won - ders are dis - played, Wher -
3. While all that bor - rows life from you Is

1. sun to rule the day; The moon shines full at
2. e'er I turn my eye: If I sur - vey the
3. ev - er in your care, And ev - ery - where that

1. his com-mand, And all the stars o - bey.
2. ground I tread, Or gaze up - on the sky!
3. man can be, You, God, are pres - ent there.

TEXT: Isaac Watts, 1674-1748, in his *Divine Songs for Children,* 1715, cento, alt.
TUNE: Melody from *Gesangbuch . . . de Herzogl Wirtembergischen katholischem Hofkapelle, Würtemberg,* 1784, arr. in *Hymns Ancient and Modern,* 1861.

The Church's One Foundation **10**

AURELIA 7.6.7.6 D

1. The Church's one foun - da - tion Is
2. E - lect from ev - 'ry na - tion, Yet
1. Je - sus Christ her Lord; She
2. one o'er all the earth, Her
1. is his new cre - a - tion By
2. char - ter of sal - va - tion, One
1. wa - ter and the word; From
2. Lord, one faith, one birth; One
1. heav'n he came and sought her To
2. ho - ly Name she bless - es, Par -
1. be his ho - ly bride;
2. takes one ho - ly food,
1. With his own blood he bought her, And
2. And to one hope she press - es, With
1. for her life he died.
2. ev - 'ry grace en - dued.

3 Though with a scornful wonder
Men see her sore opprest,
By schisms rent asunder,
By heresies distrest;
Yet saints their watch are keeping,
Their cry goes up, "How Long?"
And soon the night of weeping
Shall be the morn of song.

TEXT: Samuel John Stone, 1839-1900, in his *Lyra Fidelium,* 1866, slightly alt.
TUNE: Samuel Sebastian Wesley, 1810-1876, in Kemble's *Selection of Psalms and Hymns,* 1664.

Take My Life and Let It Be

11

SAVANNAH 77.77

1. Take my— life and let— it be
2. Take my— hands, and let— them move
3. Take my— voice, and let— me sing
4. Take my— sil - ver and— my gold,

1. Con - se - crat - ed, Lord,- to thee. Take my mo - ments
2. At the– im - pulse of— thy love. Take my feet, and—
3. Al - ways, on - ly, for— my King. Take my lips, and—
4. Not a — mite would I — with-hold. Take my in - tel -

1. and my days. Let them flow in— cease - less praise.
2. let them be Swift and beau - ti — ful for thee.
3. let them be Filled with mes - sag - es from thee.
4. lect, and use Ev - 'ry pow'r as— thou shalt choose.

5

Take my will and make it thine;
It shall be no longer mine.
Take my heart, it is thine own;
It shall be thy royal throne.

6

Take my love: my Lord, I pour
At thy feet its treasure-store.
Take myself, and I will be
Ever, only, all for thee.

TEXT: Written on 4 February 1874 by Frances Ridley Havergal, 1836-1879, first pub. in her *Royal Response*, 1878.
TUNE: German melody, © 1740, in John Wesley's *Foundery Collection*, 1742.